CANDY SHOP

CANDY SHOP

Shine J. Sun

Published by Tablo

Dear audiences,

I chose the sweetest parts from my journals, melted them, poured those into the frame, cooled them for a while, the candies are NOT STOLEN CANDIES. You'd figure out the meaning of it after savoring the poem named STOLEN CANDIES.

Your creativity is waiting to bloom, I hope it will be recognized by the people who value it.

love and peace,
Shine

p.s: I'm going to New York City in March 2020, stay there for two months, and have book talks on this book, CANDY SHOP!

Are you in? then please let me know:)

shine_sun_flower@naver.com
@shinejsun

WARNING

accidental overdose of candies (yeah, it could happen) is a leading cause of too much daydreaming. keep the candies out of reach of the people you hate. the effects of these candies may depend on how much you like daydreaming as well as other factors.

MENU

sunshine flavored candies

when you have these candies, you'll feel like you are in a wonderland. I recommend you to have these when you wanna find the door to a wonderland while you are taking a walk on a sunny day.

storm flavored candies

each storm flavored candy has a little piece of a sharp truth of life, like a photograph. it's strong enough to strike a chord. a storm flavored candy will sweep away the things that hurt you; like a storm clears the path.

snow flavored candies

like snowflakes in wintertime, they are cold. snowflake-like candies will have you recollect your sad memories. you will feel you are in the middle of the snowstorm, so bundle up before you have these candies. once they melt entirely on your heart, you'll gain the courage to face the sad memories and those memories will then never hurt you.

cloud flavored candies

like clouds flow, the stories in candies will flow too, in your mind. each candy has a fantasy-like story and as it melts in your mouth then, the stories will pop up in your mind. the stories will appear in your dream that night, in vivid ways.

SUNSHINE FLAVORED CANDIES

rainbow

red
as a sunset attached to the horizon.

orange
as a dried piece of tangerine.

yellow
as piercing sunlight at three in the afternoon.

green
as trees on a rainy day.

blue
as the outskirts of a wave in Bali.

deep blue
as the toe tip of a diver.

violet
as the opened door to a fairytale.

candy, cookie, jelly, cake

candy like cookie
cookie like candy.

jelly like cake
cake like jelly.

love like friendship
friendship like love.

where are we heading to?

the craving

his words
struck my heart.

they touched me
so hard
so i couldn't
go back
to the time bracket
before he said them.

i stayed still on the spot,
chewing his sentences
word by word.

he waited for me to digest them all,
craving my answer.

I burped,
and that meant bloody yes.

stars

the night sky bears sparkles
in its belly.

the sparkles
come down to the ground and knock on my door.

I open the door,
and through the door, they sneak into my place.

they form a huge line, and some sparkles
race against each other.

the race is held in vain
because they are all on the track of fate diving into my
bathtub and being stars.

I'll dance with those stars
but
before that
I've got to get myself ready for the dance party.

I close my eyes
and take a deep breath.

the sparkles sneak into my body.

then, they melt into
my blood vessels.

they shine, and the stars
travel through my vessels.

it aches, but not too much.

they stay for a while and leave
at just the right time
then I hear a whisper.

"now's the time to get into the bathtub."

yeah right.
the sparkles are talking to me.

I look into the mirror.

rosy cheeks,

I'm ready.

I check the temperature of the water in
the bathtub with the tip of my toe.

"yes, this is definitely the right time!"

i
dive into the tub. the sparkles
dive in right after me.

it's an endless march of sparkling moments.

thank you but...

i dripped
colored water drops
where i stood
and stepped on them.

patterns were born,
pointing out towards
where i should head.

i nodded and said thank you
to all those patterns,

walking in the opposite direction
to where they pointed.

8

instead of a night out,
we're enjoying a night in with
eight bottles of beer,
eight bottles of whiskey,
eight glasses of wine.

we'll dream all different
eight kinds of dreams this night.

someone will play the guitar
some will dance with the ghosts in their dreams.

i'll build up thick walls
to lock the noise in this room.

the sound
locked in this room
will cut the rotten
parts off
from our dreams.

then, the dream catcher will pack
its backpack to leave

because there'll be no nightmare to catch.

factory

there's a factory
in an enchanted forest.

the factory stores
somewhat weird materials—

words.

the words turn into
poems in that factory.

hundreds of
workers
work on
weaving words.

they are called the weavers.

the weavers choose the words
and design
the patterns.

but,
some weavers ignore all these rules
and create somewhat weird rugs.

doesn't matter.
they have customers
to buy those.

the threads of gold,
the threads of silver,
the threads of tears,
the threads of socks,
the threads of dwarves

these are all great materials in the factory.

what do you think?
do you have anything
to send to the factory?
if so, I'll give you its address

but,
bring enough papers.
'cause the address is not so short.

welcome to my world

i dance,
i act,
i cry,
i laugh,
and then
i repeat those all over again.

in my room
on my stage.

when your heart doesn't say yes to anything,
will you join?

Christmas

strawberries,
snowberries,
cherries,
mistletoe.
mix them all together
for a drink on
Christmas.

stolen candies

tried to steal words from other poems
but I couldn't.

crumbs of words had souls.

it seemed
they'd get crushed
like jelly
squeezed in my fist.

I stuck my ears on my heart
and tried to listen to the words
leaking from it.

they were like freshly cooked jelly
and tastier than stolen candies.

STORM FLAVORED CANDIES

the one

there are tons
of talented people out there.

you are
one of them.

not

family
is
not beautiful
not ugly.

friends
not warm
not cold.

love
not sweet
not bitter.

and i myself,
neither sane
nor perfectly insane.

instagram

the world:
be like instagram.
get to know what others like.
show them what they want to know.

me:
give me the ability to read the hashtags in them
FIRST.

passion vs. obsession

when heart bears a flame, it's passion.
when head bears a flame, it's obsession.

honey

i've got a question for you.

am I your painkiller? OR
the ultimate silver bullet? OR
the perfect cure? OR

all of these?

i

i got over you but
i haven't got over
the pain.

rusty & dusty

when you pronounce my name
in the wrong way.
it's rusty.

when you look at me
without a flame
in your eyes.
it's dusty.

sugar-coated

they grill me with
sugar-coated bitter questions.

I answer those
with my sugar-glazed words,
but the aftertaste of my words is
bitter enough to make them
to take their questions back.

sweet blood

backstabbers
wear masks
when they look for their victims.

the masks
have smiles
and look so sweet.

so, we don't get any
fishy hints
from the masks.

one way to protect ourselves is this:
wearing punching gloves
thickly coated with salt.

when you punch the backstabbers
they won't be able to tell the difference
between your punches and their tears.

plus, when blood runs out
from their noses
they could savor the taste of your punch,
their tears and blood
altogether.

peanut butter shake

one day,
I stepped into a cafe.

full of people
no seats.

so I stepped out from there.

I walked down the street,
found another cafe.

full of cookies,
no tear drops.

and I ordered
white chocolate cookies,
walnut cookies,
and chocolate chunk cookies.

a lady with
a golden smile told me,
"why don't you have a peanut butter shake?"

I nodded, and she
put a bright yellow tea coaster on my table,
served golden yellow peanut butter shake.

It was super nutty and
busted all my worries.

It blew off my dusty thoughts about him
who broke my heart.

The moment was so tasty.
The moment tasted like
the first burst of sunshine in a cave.

when i come across
what i want in my life
then i'll have peanut butter shake
to freeze it
in the sweetest way
ever.

writing

costs me my blood,
gets its inspiration from scars
requires embracing myself.

the bottom line

focus on the people who love you.
bottom line.

everyone, anyone

can't please everyone;
don't have to please anyone.

SNOW FLAVORED CANDIES

time & space

what if
i were to erase time from my life?

then no one
would ask
my age.

what if
i were to erase space from my life?

then no one
would care about
my nationality.

drama

the audiences of my life
try to define me
in their own ways
behind the silver screen.

razor

late at night
i realize that
i gotta shave off the names
that
I won't call up again
from my smartphone.

I look through them from A to Z
holding a razor in my hand.

then, I
shave off the names one by one
like I'm trimming a tree.

all the bad memories
about them, go away.

now I can get some rest
without the sound
made by the
bad memories.

deep well

I crawled up the wall
of a deep well
from the rock bottom
and it was a long journey.

the creatures I met on the wall
became my friends,
backing me up.

all of sudden,
a ladder came down from the sky
to lead me
to another rock bottom.

I looked back on my friends.

they were smiling.

not taking
my first step on the ladder,
I chose to dig a hole
in the middle of the wall.

the hole could lead me
to another rock bottom.
but at least,
I can choose the direction.

all in vain

leaves
floating in the air.

boats
floating on the water.

clouds of dust
floating on my eyeballs.

love left behind
would fade away like these.

thorn

HATE
penetrates my heart like a thorn.
it drains the blood out of my limbs.

I CAN'T STAND IT.
I'll stop it
to keep my heart alive,
even with bleeding hands.

pin

I have a pin but
can't
pin you down.

erazer

writing poems is like drawing with words,

spitting words out, i
draw lines and dots
on the hearts of the audience.

when it comes to mistakes

i
erase the lines,
erase the words,
erase the spots,
erase the specks of words.

writing poems
erases the pain and scars.

that's why I do this.

bakery

in a bakery, a mom says,
"don't lean on it."

I say to myself,
"don't lean on anyone.
stand on your own feet."

CLOUD FLAVORED CANDIES

48

pieces

we are pieces of a puzzle
in different shapes.

we don't perfectly match and
we are puzzled by that;
with puffed eyes
questioning
why all these things happen.

one time,
I thought of trimming myself
or asking you to trim yourself to fit me.

but it would not work
'cause we change over time.

so i'd say
let's just live like this.
let's leave us just like this.

my universe

i live in a universe
that I built myself
and there used to be others
living in my universe with me.

let me tell you a story.

(maybe you'd think
I'm crazy.
yes, I am.)

when mood swings
made my world swirl
I asked myself,
"Does this stem from me or
is it a plot by hormones?"

the first MYSELF answered,
"I don't know
and actually,
I'm not sure
whether it's right or wrong,
talking with you like this."

the second MYSELF said,
"don't worry,
others cannot hear
this conversation."

the third MYSELF said
"oh, come on,
you cannot open up
yourself to others.
if you do so,
the people around you
will giggle and laugh,
spicing up their words
with a sarcastic twist."

the forth MYSELF said,
"now look into my eyes
and tell me you wouldn't tell our story.
when it's released, you'll be abandoned,
like you've already been."

the fifth MYSELF said,
"your exes turned their backs on you
since you're too obsessive.
I'm the one who can give you perfect rest.
so, now you come to me."

well, you guys are begging,
but I don't wanna be with you all.
It's my turn to command something:

"oh, my universe,
burn them down."

(SILENCE)

"crush them, bend them
and melt them down,
then wash them away
till I can't see them anymore."

(SILENCE)

my universe
listened to my words
and did as I commanded.

(SILENCE)
(THUNDERING SOUND)
(SILENCE)

and I'm telling you my story
a story blocked once
by versions of myself
but now they are gone.

i
crushed them,
bent them,
melted them down to
stuck to the floor.
so, i washed them away
through the words on this page.

black day time

late at night, jazz
comes and sticks to my ears
and I fall into sleep.

the flow of music runs through my dream
then it stops
and a blank moment wakes me up.

daytime starts
even though it's dark outside.
even though it's still black,
it's daytime.

doing the laundry

when I'm scared, I think of
the fluffy puffy pillow
on my bed.

lying on my pillow on my back
scary things
melt down on my bed.

and my bed gets wet
(actually, that's my
sweat)

then, it's time
to do the laundry.

turn on the laundry machine and
the water flows out of it.

and water flushes away my mediocrity.

living a thousand lives at once

I start to count the pieces of my heart—
a thousand pieces.

violet,
naïve,
angel-like,
sweet,
hot-tempered,
mean,
trustworthy,
and so on.

I show
the mixture
of pieces to the others
and they ask me,
"who are you?"

then, I answer
"a thousand pieces are living inside me."

to give a better answer
i look into myself.

i don't know
how long it'd take
to figure out who i am.

so if you're bored,
then you can leave
anytime.

the moon

it was a full moon that I stared at
from the boat.

I was wearing glasses
and the moon didn't fit into it.

I tried to make it fit into my glasses, but soon,
I gave up. instead,
I gazed the aura of the moon
as it is.

that was enough.

a great march in March

a king passed away in March
in his twilight years.

before his death
the king had built his palace with his fellows
and had designed his tombstone.

one day, Death knocked
on the door.

Death brought a plus one.

it was Pain.

the king had one of his soldiers,
Endorphin,
to kill Pain.

the fight between
Endorphin and Pain
didn't end.

so one of the foreign soldiers,
called Morphine,
teamed up with Endorphin.

Endorphin and Morphine
almost won over Pain.

suddenly
Pain rushed to the king
and swallowed him.

several seconds passed.
with a snoring sound,
Pain threw up the king
with his body now coal black

Death said,
"now it's time to leave."
the king nodded
and followed Death.
then, Pain turned into dust
and vanished.

Endorphin and Morphine
couldn't let the king leave alone.

so they joined in the journey
to the territory of the death.

Death allowed them to join.

the king and Death,
Morphine and Endorphin
took big steps
to the palace of Death.

it was
a great march in March.

on the tombstone,
a phrase is engraved.

THE GREAT MARCH IN MARCH

it would never fade away.

I know.

I just know.

but I don't know who wrote that on
the tombstone.

the touches on that phrase
have also melted in the wind already.

honeymoon

late at night,
I take a sip of whiskey,
then
I take a trip to a deep blue ocean.

it's like a honeymoon.
an endless honeymoon.

a night is running on a treadmill
and the moon follows the track,
catching my eyes,
turning my head.

a night is running
and it never stops
while the moon is running on its track.

i savor this moment,

tasting
a scoop of honey,
tasting
a piece of the moon.

the taste of bright honey,
the scent of the sweet, sweet moon.
they all linger on my palate.

even when the morning comes,
even when the sunrise burns them down,
they'll live in my dreams.

a weird island

at the farewell party,
he said
he'd spend his vacation on a weird island,
covered with unspoken words between lovers.

I asked him
to send me a postcard filled with words
of hugs and kisses

instead of unspoken words that faded away.

a green dot

a green dot
in the pot
reflected the light of grief.

it cried
all over the night.

it woke me up,
and I asked the dot
to hold back
its tears.

it said,
"no!"

I asked,
"why?"

It said,
"If I stop crying
then the tears will overflow
inside of me choking my heart.
MY HEART WILL GET SICK!!!"

I stayed still for a minute and said,
"okay then, cry enough.
then with your tears,

I'll cook broth for all the kids in this town.
they all hold back their tears when they need to cry.
the grown-ups always stop them when they cry.

so cry.
cry enough."

then the green dot

cried and cried and cried and cried and cried and cried.
(the crying sound filled the whole kitchen)

the sound of crying blanketed the town.

the kids in the town were all awake because of the sound.

they all came to my place and cried with the green dot.

I cried and cried and cried
and cried and cried with them.

I cooked broth
with all the tear drops.

the green dot
got out of the pot,
finally.

the kids and the green dot,
sat around the table.

we savored the soup
cooked with the broth
made out of our tears.

it was a great night.

closing the door

like people come and go
emotions come and go.

let's face those emotions.
as when they're ignored
they'll hurt us
like an ingrown toe nail.

when they're recognized
they'll evaporate like cotton candy
dipped in water.

thanks to myself, my inspirations,
the ones i loved, love, and will love.

i close the door to open a new one.

Lightning Source UK Ltd.
Milton Keynes UK
UKHW010800060223
416537UK00008B/1812